The Life
of
Adam Clarke

The Life of Adam Clarke

Copyright © 2015 by Apprehending Truth.
All Rights Reserved.

ISBN-13: 978-0692585566
ISBN-10: 0692585567

Cover Design by PureLight Graphics

Apprehending Truth Publishers
PO Box 249
Brookfield, Missouri 64628

Heritage of Truth Books
is an imprint of
Apprehending Truth Publishers
http://www.ATPublishers.com

AT 10 9 8 7 6 5 4 3 2 1
151120

The Life of Adam Clarke

by

Samuel Dunn

A Heritage of Truth Book
Reclaiming the Wisdom of the Past

Apprehending Truth Publishers
Brookfield, Missouri

ADAM CLARKE LL.D. F.A.S.

THAT man is not the best Theologian who is the greatest disputant, but he who exhibits an exemplary life himself, and who teaches others to be exemplary in their lives. In things necessary to salvation, let every man become his own Theologian.

– *J. A. TURRETINE.*

THE LIFE

OF

ADAM CLARKE, LL.D., F.A.S.,

&c.

ADAM CLARKE, was born in the village of Moybeg, near Colerain, in the north of Ireland. He informed me, a short time before his death, that he had never been able to ascertain the year of his birth, his mother asserting that he was born in 1760, while his father contended that it was in 1763. Mr. John Clarke, Adam's father, was a person of very respectable literary attainments; he was educated with a view to the church, and studied successively at Edinburgh and Glasgow, where he took his degree of A.M., and afterward entered a sizar of Trinity College, Dublin, at a time when classical merit alone could gain such an admission. He was of English extraction, and Mrs. Clarke of Scottish. They had two sons and five daughters.

Adam was three years younger than his brother Tracy, and was by no means a spoiled child. He was always corrected when he deserved it, and was early inured to hardship. For this he was ever thankful, and used to say, "My heavenly Father saw that I was likely to meet with many rude blasts in journeying through life, and he prepared me in infancy for the lot his providence destined for me; so that, through his mercy, I have been enabled to carry a profitable childhood up to hoary hairs. He knew that I must walk *alone* through life, and therefore set me on my feet right early, that I might be prepared by long practice for the work I was appointed to perform." When about five years of age, he took the small pox in the natural way; but, though covered with pustules from head to foot, he was in the habit of stealing away from his *very warm* bed, whenever an opportunity presented itself, and running naked into the open air. By adopting this "*cool regimen*," he had a merciful termination of the disorder, and escaped without a single mark.

Mr. Clarke kept an English and classical school, and also held a small farm. This was cultivated by his sons, Adam and Tracy, one of whom attended to the farm, and the other at the school, alternately, during the day; and thus they shared between them the instruction which one boy in ordinary circumstances receives. They endeavoured to supply this defect by each, on leaving school, rehearsing to the other whatever he had on that day learned.

Adam was rather a dull boy, and was about eight years of age before he was capable of "putting vowels and consonants together." Having on one occasion failed again and again in his attempts to commit his task to memory, he threw down the book in despair; when the threats of his teacher, who told him he should be a beggar all his days, together with the jeers of the other scholars, roused him as from a lethargy: he felt as if something had broken within him;—his memory in a moment was all light. "What!" said he to himself, "shall I ever be a dunce, and the butt of these fellows' insults?" He resumed his book, conquered his task, speedily went up, and repeated it without missing a word, and proceeded with an ease he had never known before. He soon became passionately fond of reading. Into a wood near the school he oft retired, and there read the Eclogues and the Georgics of Virgil, with living illustrations of them before his eyes. He also amused himself with making hymns, and versifying the Psalms of David, and other portions of the sacred volume. He soon conquered the whole of the heathen mythology and biography. Of Littleton's Classical Dictionary he made himself complete master.

When but six years old, young Clarke was the subject of religious impressions. One day, as he and another little boy, with whom he was very intimate, sat upon a bank, they entered into conversation on the dreadful nature of eternal punishment. They were so affected with the thoughts that they wept bitterly; and prayed to God to forgive their sins, making mutual promises of amendment. Adam made known his feelings to his mother, and told her that he hoped in future to use no bad words, and always to obey his parents. She was deeply affected, and encouraged him and prayed for him. His parents were of different denominations; his father being a Churchman, while his mother was a Presbyterian, though not a Calvinist. To her he chiefly owed his early religions knowledge, and even his early religious impressions. It was her practice, especially on the Lord's Day, to read to her children, catechize them, and to sing and pray with them.

On one occasion, Adam having disobeyed his mother, she immediately flew to the Bible and opened on Prov. xxx, 17, which she read and commented on in the most awful manner: "The eye that mocketh at his father, and despiseth to obey his mother, the ravens of the valley shall pick it out, and the young eagles shall eat it." He was cut to the heart, thinking the words were immediately sent from heaven! He went out into the field much distressed, and was musing on this terrible denunciation of the divine displeasure, when the hoarse croak of a raven sounded to his conscience an alarm more terrible than the cry of fire at midnight. He looked up, and soon perceived this most ominous bird; and actually supposing it the raven of which the text spoke, coming to pick out his eyes, he clapped his hands on them with the utmost speed and trepidation and ran toward the house as fast as his state of salutary fright and perturbation would permit, that he might escape the impending vengeance!

He was sent by his parents to a singing school, where, after a while, he received instructions in dancing as well as music. Of this seductive art he soon became exceedingly fond; and says that he found it to be a perverting influence, an unmixed moral evil; and, to his death, on all proper occasions, he lifted up his voice against this branch of fashionable education.

In the year 1777, the Methodist preachers visited the parish in which the Clarke family resided. Adam went to hear them; and, under their preaching, especially under that of Mr. Thomas Barber, his mind became enlightened to see his danger, and he earnestly desired to flee from the wrath to come. His former evil courses were abandoned, his old companions forsaken, and he began to meet in class.

After a long night of sorrow, the day of deliverance drew near; and never shall I forget the feeling with which, about ten years ago, he related this part of his religious experience in a party of friends, among whom were several young persons not decidedly religious, for whose benefit, as he informed me afterward, he then entered so largely into the circumstances that attended his conversion. He described the field to which he went with a conscience heavily burdened with guilt, the spot on which he kneeled and wrestled with God in prayer till his strength was exhausted. The heavens appeared as brass; he found no access to the throne of grace. Concluding that there was no mercy for him, he at last rose in despair, intending "to cease the agonizing strife." On retiring from the place he heard, or thought he heard, a voice, which said to him, "Try Jesus!" He was not disobedient, but immediately went back to the same spot, there called upon Jesus, and his sorrow was instantly turned into joy. A glow of happiness seemed to thrill through his whole frame; all guilt and condemnation were gone. He examined his conscience, and found it no longer a register of sins against God. He looked to heaven, and all was sunshine. He searched for his distress, but could not find it. His heart was light, his physical strength and his animal spirits returned, and he could, more nimbly than ever, bound like a roe. He felt a sudden transition from darkness to light, from guilt and oppressive fear to confidence and peace. He could now draw nigh to God with more confidence than he ever could to his earthly father: he had freedom of access, and he had freedom of speech.

With this gladness of soul he also received great intellectual enlargement. He could prosecute his literary studies with much greater ease. He now learned more in one day than formerly he was able to do in one month. His mind became enlarged to take in any thing useful. He saw that religion was the gate to true learning and science; and soon began, in addition to his other pursuits, to apply himself to astronomy, natural philosophy, and the mathematics.

His parents at first designed him for the church, and afterward for the medical profession; but the narrowness of their pecuniary resources presented innumerable obstacles, which they were unable to surmount. It was then concluded that he should become a schoolmaster; but for this he had no inclination. He was at last sent to Mr. Francis Bennett, a linen merchant, of Colerain, a kinsman of his parents, who had proposed to take him on advantageous terms.

It should here be mentioned that the subject of this memoir, in his boyhood, had two very narrow escapes from sudden death: the one was a severe fall from a horse, when a sack of grain, which he had been unable to balance on the animal, came down with all its force upon him; and, his back happening to come in contact with a pointed stone, he was taken up apparently dead. In about four-and- twenty hours he was conveyed home, and in a short time completely restored. His second escape was from being drowned; he having imprudently, in riding for the purpose of washing his father's mare in an armlet of the sea, taken her out of her depth, till they were carried beyond the breakers into the swell, where they were both swamped in a moment. But that God whom "waves obey," and who designed him for matters of great and high importance, caused one wave after another to perform for him the genial service of rolling him to the shore before the vital spark was quite extinct.

The love of God was no sooner shed abroad in his heart, than he felt a yearning pity, a burning charity, for his friends and fellow creatures. He not only induced his parents to have family worship, on the morning and evening of every day in the week, as well as on the Sabbath, which they had been accustomed to have; but he also consented, though it was a heavy cross, regularly to officiate himself. He, however, had his reward: all his relatives became hearers of the Methodists, and most of them members of society. He then began to exhort his neighbours to turn to God. On the Sabbath he went regularly, in all weathers, a distance of more than six miles to meet a class, which assembled so early that, in the winter, he had to set out two hours before day. When he had met his class, he proceeded to the nearest village, and entering the first open door, said, "Peace be to this house!" If consent was given, he called in the neighbours, prayed, and gave a short exhortation. This done, he went to another village, and repeated the same plan; and so on through the day, without ever encountering a direct refusal. His youth and great seriousness made a favourable impression, which his prayers and exhortations tended to deepen. In this manner he not unfrequently visited nine or ten villages in one day.

After his removal to Colerain, he and his master went on for some time very comfortably, and Mr. Bennett was much pleased with him. To Mr. Henry Moore, who was personally acquainted with Mr. Bennett, we are indebted for the following information: "Mr. Bennett and young Clarke were one day engaged in measuring a piece of linen, preparatory to the great market in Dublin. They found *that* particular piece wanting some inches of a yard at the end. 'Come, Adam,' says Mr. Bennett, 'lay hold, and pull against me; and we shall soon make it come up to the yard.' But he little knew with whom he had to deal. Adam dropped the linen on the ground, and stood and looked like one benumbed. 'What's the matter?' said Mr. Bennett. 'Sir,' he replied, 'I can't do it: I think it is a wrong thing.' Mr. Bennett urged that it was done every day; that it would not make the linen any the worse; and that the process through which it had passed had made it shrink a little; and concluded by bidding him take hold! 'No,' says Adam, 'no!' Mr. Bennett was a very placid man, and they entered calmly into dispute. At last he was obliged to give it up; Adam would not consent to meddle with it; he thought it was not fair. It did not suit the standard of his conscience." He continued with Mr. Bennett about one year, without being bound an apprentice, and then parted with him in the most friendly manner.

Shortly after this, he received an invitation to visit Mr. Bredin, one of the preachers, then on the Londonderry side of the circuit. The day after his arrival Mr. Bredin desired him to preach, and take a text. This he had not yet attempted, and, being alive to its importance, objected; but his friend persisting strongly to urge him, he at length yielded, and preached his first sermon at New Buildings, a village five miles from Derry, June 19, 1782, from 1 John v. 19: "We know that we are of God, and the whole world lieth in wickedness." The generality of his hearers were so well pleased that they entreated him to preach to them the next morning at five. He consented, and during his short stay preached five times. Mr. Bredin, believing that his young friend was called of God to the work of the ministry, wrote to Mr. Wesley concerning him, who immediately offered to take Adam into Kingswood School, near Bristol. When this proposal was communicated to his parents, they were quite indignant. His father would neither speak to him nor see him. His mother told him that, if he left them, he would go with her curse, and not her blessing. He had recourse to the throne of grace, and God heard him. His parents became convinced that he had other work to do, and granted him their permission to leave them. He sailed from Londonderry on the 17th of August, 1782; taking with him, as provision for the voyage, a loaf of bread and a pound of cheese, and reached Liverpool in two days. He travelled by coach to Bristol; and the next morning, August 25th, with only three halfpence in his pocket, walked to Kingswood.

The treatment he received while here, from the head master and his wife, was most unkind, and just the reverse of that which he had expected; but it lasted only one month and two days,—thirty-one days too much, if God had not been pleased to order it otherwise. Mr. Wesley, however, returned in a few weeks from Cornwall, and then sent for Adam. "I went into Bristol," says he, "saw Mr. Rankin, who carried me to Mr. Wesley's study, off the great lobby of the rooms over the chapel in Broadmead. He tapped at the door, which was opened by this truly apostolic man; Mr. Rankin retired. Mr. Wesley took me kindly by the hand, and asked me how long since I had left Ireland. Our conversation was short. He said, 'Well, brother Clarke, do you wish to devote yourself entirely to the work of God?' I answered, 'Sir, I wish to do and be what God pleases!' He then said, 'We want a preacher for Bradford; (Wilts.); hold yourself in readiness to go thither; I am going into the country, and will let you know when you shall go.' He then turned to me, laid his hands upon my head, and spent a few moments in praying to God to bless and preserve me, and to give me success in the work to which I was called."

Mr. Clarke entered on the regular work of a

Methodist travelling preacher, on September 26th, 1782, having a tolerable acquaintance with the Scriptures and a heart full of zeal for the salvation of souls; and though he had the appearance of a "little boy," yet he was so prudent and deeply serious, that "no man despised his youth." Souls were awakened, and many young persons especially began earnestly to inquire the way of salvation. The circuit was very extensive, comprising no less than thirty- one towns and villages, and he had to preach and travel several miles every day, beside attending to various other duties; yet such was his thirst for learning, that he availed himself of every opportunity for cultivating his mind, by rising early, reading on horseback, and "never whiling away his time." But a circumstance took place about this period which had nearly proved ruinous to all his attainments in literature. In the preachers' room at Motcomb, near Shaftesbury, observing a Latin sentence on the wall, he wrote another from Virgil, corroborative of the first. One of his colleagues, Mr. J. A., subjoined, "Did you write the above to show us you could write Latin? For shame! Do send pride to hell, from whence it came. O young man! Improve your time! Eternity's at hand." This ridiculous effusion, probably the offspring of envy, had such an effect on the mind of Mr. Clarke, that in a moment of strong temptation he fell on his knees in the midst of the room, and solemnly promised to God that he would never more meddle with Greek or Latin as long as he lived! This hasty vow he observed for four years, when he bitterly repented of it, asked forgiveness of God, and recommenced the study of these languages.

During this year he read Mr. Wesley's "Letter on Tea," and resolved that he would drink neither tea nor coffee, till he could answer the arguments to his satisfaction. This resolution he kept to the end of his life.

At the following conference he was admitted into full connection, and then appointed to the Norwich circuit, which at that time extended over considerable portions of Norfolk and Suffolk. Religion was at an exceedingly low ebb; and scarcely a Sabbath passed without disturbances at the Methodist chapel. During a remarkably severe winter he endured many hardships, often sleeping in lofts and outhouses, and being obliged to subsist on very scanty fare.

From Norwich he went in the year 1784 to St. Austell, in Cornwall, which was also a very heavy circuit; the places were numerous, and he had to preach almost every week in the year in the open air, and at times too when the rain was pouring down, and when the snow lay deep upon the ground. "But the prosperity of Methodism made every thing pleasant." A heavenly flame broke out, and great numbers joined the society. Among these was Samuel Drew, who was then just terminating his apprenticeship to a shoemaker: "A man," says Mr. Clarke, "of primitive simplicity of manners, amiableness of disposition, piety toward God, and benevolence to men, seldom to be equaled; and for reach of thought, keenness of discrimination, purity of language, and manly eloquence, not to be surpassed in any of the common walks of life. In short, his circumstances considered, with the mode of his education, he is one of those prodigies of nature and grace which God rarely exhibits; but which serve to keep up the connecting link between those who are confined to houses of clay, whose foundations are in the dust, and beings of a superior order in those realms where infirmity cannot enter, and where the sunshine of knowledge suffers neither diminution nor eclipse." Eulogistic as this is, I can bear testimony to its correctness. I knew Mr. Drew well, received many a useful lesson from him, esteemed him while he lived, and now deeply revere his memory. I have frequently heard him and my venerable father, with other aged Methodists in my native circuit, speak of Mr. Clarke's unbounded popularity in those early days; he being sometimes obliged, when the chapel had been thronged, to enter through the window, and creep on his hands and knees over the heads and shoulders of the people, in order to reach the pulpit. The doctor's death was a severe stroke to Mr. Drew; he survived it only a few months; they were then joined

> "In those Elysian seats
> Where Jonathan his David meets."

In 1785 Mr. Clarke was appointed to Plymouth Dock, (now called Devonport,) where the society was doubled in the course of the year. Here Chambers' Cyclopaedia, in two volumes folio, was lent him by James Hore, Esq. He read it attentively, made nearly every subject discussed in it his own; and laid the whole under contribution to his ministerial labours. He also obtained the loan from Miss Kennicott, of her brother's (the celebrated Dr. Kennicott's) edition of the Hebrew Bible, two volumes folio, with various readings from near seven hundred MSS. and early printed editions. This book greatly increased his thirst for a better knowledge of biblical criticism.

The next three years were spent in the Norman Isles. Here he obtained much assistance from the public library of St. Heliers, where he spent most of his leisure hours in reading and collating the original texts in Walton's Polyglot Bible, particularly the Hebrew, Samaritan, Chaldee, Syriac, Vulgate, and Septuagint: and before he left, he was enabled to purchase a Polyglot for himself, with ten pounds which he had received in a letter from a person from whom he had no expectation of receiving any thing of the kind. But what was more pleasing to him, the word of the Lord had free course and was glorified. Among the converts was a soldier who had been a slave to drunkenness. One morning, having become intoxicated before five o'clock, he had strolled out to Les Torres, where Mr. Clarke was preaching, and was deeply convinced of his lost condition. At the close of the service, he took Mr. Clarke by the hand, and with the tears streaming down his cheeks, between drunkenness and distress, said, "O sir! I know you are a man possessed by the Spirit of God!" He went home; and after three days' agonies, God, in tender compassion, set his soul at liberty.

While on this station he had several very remarkable deliverances: once or twice from the hands of a furious mob; another time from the fatal effects of intense cold, while walking through deep snow; and once from a watery grave, while in a little vessel, during a tremendous storm, off Alderney.

On the 17th of April, 1788, Mr. Clarke was married to Miss Mary Cooke, the eldest daughter of

Mr. John Cooke, clothier, Trowbridge. In a private communication he says, "Before I took my beloved Mary by the hand, who was most delicately brought up, I asked her, 'As I am at the disposal of Mr. Wesley and the conference, and they can send me whither they please, will you go with me whithersoever I am sent?' 'Yes; if I take you, I take you as a minister of Christ, and shall go with you to the ends of the earth.' And the first step she took was with me on my mission to the Norman Isles." It is only necessary to say that, for above forty-two years, during which they were united, she showed, in all the various circumstances through which they passed, she was the woman worthy of being the wife of Adam Clarke. Six sons and six daughters were the fruit of their marriage. Miss Anne Cooke, one of Mrs. Clarke's sisters, became the wife of John Butterworth, Esq., and, with her husband, was brought to God through Mr. and Mrs. Clarke's instrumentality, and for many years, in a very elevated station, adorned the doctrine of God their Saviour in all things.

In 1789 Mr. Clarke received his appointment as superintendent for the Bristol circuit. This, in consequence of family afflictions and other causes, he informed me, was one of the most painful years of his life.

The conference of 1790 appointed him to

Dublin[1], where he no sooner arrived than he found himself exposed to numberless difficulties and distressing circumstances. He and his family were obliged to go into very inconvenient lodgings; and when the preacher's new house was finished, they were induced to go into it before it was dry, which nearly cost all of them their lives. He was seized with a severe rheumatic affection in the head, from which he very slowly recovered. There were also

---

[1] He had previously received the following letter from Mr. Wesley:—

"Near Dublin, June 25, 1789.

"Dear Adam,

"You send me good news with regard to the islands. Who can hurt us, if God is on our side? Trials may come, but they are all good. I have not been so tried for many years. Every week, and almost every day, I am bespattered in the public papers. Many are in tears on the occasion, many terribly frightened, and crying out, 'O, what will the end be? What will the end be?' Why, glory to God in the highest, and peace and good will among men. But, meantime, what is to be done? What will be the most effectual means to stem this furious torrent? I have just visited the classes, and find still in the society upward of a thousand members; and, among them, many as deep Christians as any I have met with in Europe. But who is able to watch over these that they may not be moved from their steadfastness? I know none more proper than Adam Clarke and his wife. Indeed, it may seem hard for them to go into a strange land again. Well, you may come to me, at Leeds, the latter end of next month; and if you can show me any that are more proper, I will send them instead, that God may be glorified in all that is designed by,

"Dear Adam,
"Your affectionate friend and brother,
"J. Wesley."

very warm disputes in the society, respecting the use of the liturgy in the Whitefriar-street Chapel, which gave him great uneasiness. While in this circuit he formed a charitable institution, called "The Strangers' Friend Society," the first of several that were organized by him in the principal towns of England, as Manchester, Liverpool, and London; and which have contributed greatly to the relief of suffering humanity.

The year 1791 is remarkable in the history of Methodism for the death of Mr. Wesley. When Mr. Clarke first heard of this solemn event, he says that he "was overwhelmed with grief; and that such were his feelings, all he could do was to read the little printed account of his last moments." His admiration of Mr. Wesley was such as I have not perceived in any other of the followers of that extraordinary individual. I have more than once heard him say, that, taking him altogether, as a man, a Christian, a divine, a philanthropist, a favoured instrument in the hands of God in winning souls, he had not been surpassed, if equalled, since the days of the apostles. It is deeply to be regretted that peculiar circumstances should have prevented the doctor from writing the Life of the Founder of Methodism,—an Apelles that could have painted an Alexander. Mr. Wesley's opinion of Mr. Clarke we have in a letter of his to Mr. King. So early as the year 1787, that correct judge of character hesitated not to affirm, "Adam Clarke is doubtless an extraordinary young man, and capable of doing much good." In his will, Mr. Wesley appointed him one of the seven trustees of all his literary property.

The first conference after the death of Mr. Wesley, as Mr. Clarke's health was in a very declining state, he was appointed to the Manchester circuit, principally with a view to his using the Buxton waters, as the likeliest means of his recovery. The remedy was tried, and his health completely restored. About this time the French revolution was the universal topic; and various political questions were agitated with considerable excitement. These were sometimes introduced into the pulpit, but never by Mr. Clarke: he informed me that, during this painful period, in almost every sermon he urged his hearers to seek entire sanctification. Of his colleagues, Messrs. Samuel Bradburn and Joseph Benson, I have heard him speak in the highest terms. He thought them the two greatest preachers of the day. It is somewhat remarkable that it fell to his lot to perform the last office of friendship to the mortal remains of both these eminent men, by delivering an address at their graves. The former died in 1810, the latter in 1821.

From Manchester Mr. Clarke went to Liverpool, where he and the venerable Mr. Pawson, with whom he acted in perfect unison, had the satisfaction of seeing the society more than doubled during their joint ministry. Mrs. Pawson then entered, in her private journal, her opinion of her husband's colleague in the following terms:— "Brother Clarke is, in my estimation, an extraordinary preacher; and his learning confers great lustre on his talents: he makes it subservient to grace. His discourses are highly evangelical: he never loses sight of Christ. In regard of pardon and holiness, he offers a present salvation. His address is lively, animated, and very encouraging to the seekers of salvation. In respect to the unawakened, it may indeed be said, that he obeys that precept, 'Cry aloud; spare not; lift up thy voice like a trumpet.' His words flow spontaneously from the heart; his views enlarge as he proceeds; and he brings to the mind a torrent of things new and old. While he is preaching, one can seldom cast an eye on the audience, without perceiving a melting unction resting upon them. His 'speech distils as the dew, and as the small rain upon the tender herb.' He generally preaches from some part of the lesson for the day; and, on the Sabbath morning, from the Gospel for the day: this method confers an abundant variety on his ministry."

While in this circuit, Mr. Clarke nearly lost his life by assassination. Returning home one evening from a country village accompanied by two friends, a stone, upward of a pound weight, struck him on the head, cut through his hat, and inflicted a deep wound. This horrid deed was proved to be the act of a Papist, who, with another of the same creed, had been to hear him preach, and waylaid him on his return; and, had he been alone, would in all probability have murdered him. He was confined for more than a month, a considerable part of which time his life was in great jeopardy. The men were brought before a magistrate; but, on their confessing their fault, and binding themselves never more to offend, both of them were discharged,—though in a few years they both came to a tragical end.

The next three years Mr. Clarke spent in London, and during that time walked upward of seven thousand miles, merely in the performance of his duty as a Methodist preacher. In the year 1797 he commenced his career of authorship by the publication of a pamphlet, entitled, "A Dissertation on the Use and Abuse of Tobacco."

From the year 1798 to 1805 the subject of our memoir was appointed successively to Bristol, Liverpool, and Manchester. His father died in November, 1798, full of faith and hope. This he laid deeply to heart, and expressed himself as if the hands of life were loosened around him, and that he wished to "go and die with him." He never afterward passed Ardwick churchyard, where his father was interred, without taking off his hat, and holding it in his hand until he had made his way beyond it, to manifest how much he honored, as well as loved, this guide of his youth.

In the year 1800, Mr. Clarke published a translation of "Sturm's Reflections on the Works of God," which had an extensive and rapid sale.

In 1802 he edited and published "A Bibliographical Dictionary," in 6 vols., to which, in the year 1806, he added two other volumes, as a "Bibliographical Miscellany or Supplement;" and, about the same time, "A Succinct Account of Polyglot Bibles, from the publication of that by Porrus in the year 1516, to that of Reineccius in 1750: including several curious particulars relative to the London Polyglot, and Castell's Heptaglott Lexicon, not noticed by Bibliographers:" also, "A Succinct Account of the principal Editions of the Greek Testament, from the first printed at Complutum, in 1514, to that by Professor Griesbach, in 1797." These several works contain a mass of information, and will be found a useful guide to the study of Biblical literature.

While in Liverpool Mr. Clarke projected the

formation of a "Philological Society;" of which he was unanimously chosen president. The same honour was conferred upon him a few years after, when a similar society was instituted in Manchester. The code of rules, and one hundred and seventy-one questions on various literary and scientific subjects came from the pen of Mr. Clarke. A copy of them now lies before me. Some of the questions are exceedingly important and curious.

In 1804 Mr. Clarke gave to the public an improved edition of "Fleury's Manners of the Ancient Israelites;" and an abridgment of "Baxter's Christian Directory," in 2 vols. During the same year, the Eclectic Review was commenced; and Mr. Clarke was earnestly requested to lend his able assistance in reviewing some Hebrew and other oriental works. After some reluctance he consented, and furnished some reviews, which contributed not a little to the respectability of the new periodical. Of his review of Holmes' Septuagint, Professor Bentley writes, "It is more conformable to my ideas of what a review should be, than is generally to be met with in the periodical publications of the present day: it is such a complete account and analysis of the work and will enable a person to form a just opinion of it. The article contains many particulars of additional information, more than Holmes has given; and these you have so intermingled with those drawn from Holmes, that the generality of readers will not perceive to whom they are indebted for them. The opposite to this is, I believe, the usual practice of reviewers: they often display information as their own, which they owe altogether to their author, whom they perhaps are abusing; and thus make it more their object to seem *knowing* themselves than even to give a proper and just account of the author whose work they are professing to review."

He was appointed a second time to the London circuit in 1805; and, at the conference held in Leeds in 1806, he was elected president; and, in defiance of all his protestations against it, he was taken by main force, lifted out of his seat, and placed in the chair!

About this time "the British and Foreign Bible Society" nominated Mr. Clarke a member of its committee. The assistance which he rendered was most important, such as "was indispensable to the successful prosecution of the society's plans," and which cost him no ordinary sacrifice of time and labour. For it the committee requested permission to present him with fifty pounds; "an offering," says the late Rev. John Owen, "which that learned and public-spirited individual respectfully but peremptorily declined to accept."

His "Concise View of the Succession of Sacred

Literature" made its appearance in 1807. For the completion of the second volume of this valuable work the doctor could never find leisure; but this, and a new and enlarged edition of the first, in 8vo., have been finished and published by the doctor's youngest son, the Rev. J. B. B. Clarke, A.M., in a manner highly creditable to his scholarship and talents.

In the same year the University of Aberdeen, at the suggestion of the celebrated Professor Porson, conferred on Mr. Clarke the degree of A.M.; and, in the following year, presented him with a diploma of LL.D. Both diplomas were sent to him in the most honourable and flattering manner, the college refusing to accept even the customary clerks' fees given on such occasions.

"Some time in February, 1808," he observes, "I learned that I had been recommended to his majesty's commissioners of the public records of the kingdom, by the Right Honourable Charles Abbot, speaker of the house of commons, and one of the commissioners, to whom I was known only by some of my writings on Bibliography, as a fit person to undertake the department of collecting and arranging those state papers which might serve to complete and continue that collection of state papers generally called *Rymer's Faedora.*" He was struck with astonishment, and endeavoured to excuse himself on the grounds of general unfitness. But being strongly urged by John Caley, Esq., secretary to the commission, and some of his friends, to try, he commenced this Herculean task. He had to examine sixty folio volumes, with numerous collateral evidence, to visit the different public offices, and to make a selection of such records as it might be expedient to print, under the authority of parliament, either as a supplement or continuation of Rymer's work. These excessive labours[2] tended greatly to impair his health, until he was obliged, on three different occasions, to send in his resignation to the "board:" it was not, however, accepted before March, 1819; when he took leave of this part of his public duties in the following language: "And here I register my thanks to God, the Fountain of wisdom and goodness, who has enabled me to conduct this most difficult and delicate work for ten years, with credit to myself, and satisfaction to his majesty's government. During that time I have been requested to solve many difficult questions, and illustrate many obscurities; in none of which have I ever failed, though the subjects were such as were by no means

---

[2] In a letter to myself, he says, "Lord Glenbervie, who was one of the commissioners, once wrote to me: 'Dr. Clarke, *festina lente:* you will destroy yourself by your labour. Do a little, that you may do it long.' The same advice I give you. May God bless you, my dear Sammy."

familiar to me, having had little of an antiquarian, and nothing of a forensic education."

In 1808, Dr. Clarke was prevailed upon to become librarian of the Surrey Institution; and when he relinquished the office, the managers, as a mark of respect, constituted him "honorary librarian;" which title he retained as long as the institution existed. In the course of the same year he published A Short Account of the last Illness and Death of the learned Porson, with a *facsimile* of an ancient Greek inscription, which formed the topic of the professor's last literary conversation.

In the year 1810, Dr. Clarke projected, in conjunction with the Rev. Josiah Pratt, a new edition of the London Polyglot Bible. The prospectus was printed and circulated, but, for want of adequate support, the important undertaking was abandoned. This he greatly regretted to the day of his death. It was in the month of July of this year that the first part of his Commentary on the Holy Scriptures was issued from the press. This monument of learning and piety we shall afterward notice.

On the 1st of December, 1814, a Wesleyan Methodist missionary meeting was held for the first time in City-Road Chapel, London. Dr. Clarke, being that year president of the conference, was called to the chair; and shortly after published the address which he delivered, under the title of "A Short Account of the Introduction of the Gospel into the British Isles; and the Obligation of Britons to make known its Salvation to every Nation of the Earth."

In 1815, Dr. Clarke removed from London, and took up his residence at Millbrook, in Lancashire. Here he was relieved from many burdens that in the metropolis had pressed heavily upon him, breathed a pure air, and engaged himself in his favourite agricultural pursuits, which had a most beneficial effect upon his constitution. In the summer of 1816, he made a tour through part of Scotland and Ireland, and visited what he calls, in a letter now before me, "the place that had every thing to recommend it to *my attention and heart.* The place is that in which I spent my boyish days; where I received the rudiments of the little education I have; where I first felt conviction of sin, righteousness, and judgment; where I first saw or heard a Methodist; where I first tasted the pardoning love of God, after having passed through a great fight of affliction; where I joined the Methodist society; where I first led a class; where I first began to preach redemption in Christ Jesus, and from which I was called to become an itinerant preacher. And these things took place in the parish, and in the compass of about three fields' breadth in that parish, which is on the edge of the sea, where there is the most beautiful shore in the world, extending above twenty miles, of as perfectly level hard sand as can be conceived;—the very place where

I was once drowned, and perhaps *miraculously* restored to life; where I was accustomed to bathe, and from the rocks of which I used to catch many fish, and among the rocks of which I spent many an hour in catching crabs, &c. Such a place, thus circumstanced, must afford a multitude of the most impressive reminiscences. No place on the face of the earth can have so many attractions for *me.*"

Dr. Clarke came to town in May, 1818, to attend the anniversary meetings of the Wesleyan Methodist Missionary Society; and, while on the platform, he received a note from Sir Alexander Johnston, who was then within sight of land, on his return from Ceylon, and who had brought with him, at their own most earnest entreaties, two high priests of Budhoo, who wished to be instructed in the principles of Christianity. Sir Alexander and the missionary committee prevailed on Dr. Clarke to take charge of them, and afford them all the instructions he could in the knowledge of divine things. Two days after their arrival in London, I had the pleasure of accompanying the doctor and these two interesting strangers, one of whom was then forty-five years of age, and the other twenty-seven, to Bristol. They travelled without hat or cap, with a splendid yellow garment thrown loosely over the left shoulder, and with not only the head, but also the neck, breast, and right arm entirely bare, to the no little astonishment of beholders. They remained with their kind and eminent instructor for about two years, were baptized into the Christian faith, and then returned to Ceylon, where they have held fast their profession. One fills an important office under government, and the other is a licensed teacher in the Church establishment.

In June, 1821, the doctor again visited Ireland, and, shortly after, his name was enrolled among the chief literati of the country. In a letter to me he writes:

"M.R.I.A. signify *Member of the Royal Irish Academy,* to which I was most honourably elected, without knowing any of the parties who brought me before the Academy; my countrymen being determined to bestow on me the highest literary honour in their gift."

In the spring of the following year an acquaintance was commenced between Dr. Clarke and his royal highness the duke of Sussex. This was most honourable to the doctor, was unsolicited on his part, and continued without any compromise of either his character or principles.

At the conference held in London in the year 1822, Dr. Clarke was, for the third time, chosen president; a circumstance as yet unique in the history of Methodism. It was determined at this conference that two preachers should be sent to the Shetland Isles. The writer of these lines, who was present on the occasion, was the first who offered his services, if his brethren thought him adequate for the arduous enterprise. He was immediately appointed; and, with the Rev. John Ruby, after spending a few days at Millbrook, proceeded to Edinburgh, there took ship, and, after four days' sail, safely arrived in Lerwick. In the name of the Lord of hosts they set up their banner; they preached a free, full, and present salvation; multitudes flocked to hear the word, and not a few felt its transforming efficacy. Other preachers followed in the same track, and were equally successful. From ten to twenty chapels have been erected, and numerous societies formed. There are now six Wesleyan Methodist preachers labouring in the islands, and one thousand three hundred and seventy members in society. What the mission to these "naked melancholy isles" is indebted to Dr. Clarke, will not be known before "that day shall break which never more shall close." He travelled, he begged, he wrote, he prayed for it; and it is my decided conviction that, without his very efficient aid, such as no other man in the kingdom could have rendered, it would have been long since abandoned. Of that assistance it is now deprived, and is dependent for its support on the Methodists' Contingent Fund, and on the contributions of an enlightened and benevolent public. I most strongly, therefore, recommend it to the attention and liberality of all who revere the memory of the venerable doctor, or who feel compassion for the sheep that are scattered over the mountains.[3]

The doctor visited the islands himself in the year 1826, and again in 1827; and on his return, when I was stationed in Newcastle-on-Tyne, wrote to me thus: "And now, Sammy, what shall I say about the *work* of which we have written and spoken so much? I cannot say that it *answered* my expectation. It *far exceeded* all that I had even hoped. I have not witnessed so much good done in so short a time, with such slender means, wherever I have travelled; nor have I read of such. I saw all the preachers, and had the leaders from every isle and place of preaching, (either at Walls or Lerwick,) and I inquired closely into the work everywhere; and I believe I pretty well know the whole; I have seen the grace of God which is among them, and am

---

[3] Subscriptions and donations will be thankfully received by the amiable relict of the Doctor, Mrs. Clarke, Stoke Newington, or by any of the Wesleyan Ministers.

sovereignly glad. The half of the good I witnessed had not been told me. Indeed, the preachers themselves do not fully know it. When I reflected on *your first entering in* among this people, the difficulties which you had to encounter, the soil wholly unprepared, I stand astonished at the work. I see fully that of the great harvest in the principal parts of Shetland, *you* sowed the seed. God has put great honour upon you, and multitudes remember you even with tears of affection."

It was in the year 1824 that Dr. Clarke sold his house and land in Lancashire, quitted Millbrook, and purchased, and then removed to Haydon Hall, a lovely spot, near Pinner, and about sixteen miles from London.

In 1830, the doctor, on his visit to Ireland, established several schools in the extensive and populous districts around Colerain, where many were perishing for lack of knowledge. These schools were inspected by him in 1831.

In January, 1830, he gave the following account of the death of Robert Scott, Esq., of Pensford, near Bristol, in a letter to Mrs. Clarke: "At half past ten this evening, Mr. Scott changed mortality for life. Such a death I never witnessed. We had prayed to God to give him an easy passage; and we did not pray in vain: for he had one of the most placid and easiest I have ever heard or seen.

His wife, and several of the relatives, and myself were kneeling around his bed. I offered the departing prayer; and, after it, had just time to rise from my knees, to go to him, lay my hands on his head, and pronounce the blessing of Aaron on the Israelites:

'The Lord bless thee, and keep thee! The Lord make his face shine upon thee, and be gracious unto thee! The Lord lift up his countenance upon thee, and give thee peace,' when his last breath went forth! Thus, in the eighty-fifth year of his age, died this undeviating friend of Shetland I would not have missed this sight for a great deal. I seem to have come hither in order to learn to die."

The following letter I received in 1825:—

"MY DEAR SAMMY,

"When I had but one sovereign in the world for Shetland, I prayed, called earnestly upon God, and sat down and wept—and wept till I could scarcely see to write or read. Well, I once more thought, I must lay the whole before our best earthly friend. With a full heart, I stated the matter in a letter to Mr. Scott, which letter was watered with fast falling tears. He wrote me word that he and Mrs. Scott would be up in a fortnight and see me. They came; and I set off in very bad health to London to meet them:—and O, what a meeting!—their hearts were nearly as full as mine. Says Mr. Scott, 'Come, let me have a check, I will give orders on my bank for £100.' Says Mrs. Scott, 'And I will, out of my private purse, give £5?' 'And I am desired,' says Mr. Scott, 'by my sister-in-law, Miss Grainger, to give £5; and lest any chapel begun should be impeded, here is £10 more, and thus I will give the check for £120. And this is not all that I will do; I tell you again, I will give £10 to every chapel or house begun under your direction in Shetland.' O, my Sammy! you can hardly tell how much I rejoiced—I thanked God, I thanked them, and could have kissed the ground on which they trod. I said in my heart, 'O my poor Shetlanders! (whom I have never seen, and now never shall see, but God has laid you upon my heart) God has not forgotten you.' I sent my check to the bankers, got the cash, £120, and immediately wrote to you, and told you what God had done, to take courage and go forward. Mr. Scott has written to me, two or three days ago, stating that he is very poorly, and wishes to make a 'trust deed' in behalf of Shetland, and to do this immediately; and wishes me to give him the names with which I wish it to be filled. Old as I am, I must be one, Mr. Butterworth will be another, and you shall be the third.

"Yours, my dear Sammy, affectionately,
"ADAM CLARKE"

Mr. Butterworth, Mr. Scott, and the dear doctor, have all since been called to give an account of their stewardship. Mr. Scott left three thousand pounds to the Shetland mission, in the three-and-half per cents.

On his return to Haydon-Hall, he found a letter containing an invitation from the board of managers of the Missionary Society of the

Methodist Episcopal Church of New-York, to go over to America, and assist them in their missionary labours, and in their church assembly. After stating the reasons why he could not accept the invitation, and expressing his regret, he proceeds thus: "Yet I am far from supposing that there may not be a providential interference in the way. I am an old man, having gone beyond threescore years and ten, and, consequently, not able to perform the labour of youth. You would naturally expect me to preach much; and this I could not do . . . . I would say to all, Keep your doctrines and your discipline, not only in your church books, and in your society rules, but preach the former without refining upon them, observe the latter without bending it to circumstances, or impairing its rigour by frivolous exceptions and partialities. As I believe your nation to be destined to be the mightiest and happiest nation on the globe, so I believe that your church is likely to become the most extensive and pure in the universe. As a church, abide in the apostles' doctrine and fellowship. As a nation, be firmly united; entertain no petty differences; totally abolish the slave trade; abhor all offensive wars; never provoke even the puniest state; and never strike the first blow. Encourage agriculture and friendly traffic. Cultivate the sciences and arts; let learning have its proper place, space, and adequate share of esteem and honour. If possible, live in peace with all nations; retain your holy zeal for God's cause and your country's weal; and that you may ever retain yore' liberty, avoid, as its bane and ruin, a national debt."

In May, 1832, he visited Ireland for the last time; and in a private communication gives the following account of his voyage:—"On Tuesday, I left Bruerton in the mail for Liverpool, where I arrived at six in the evening; immediately crossed the Mersey, and got to Oakfield, to my old friend, Mr. Forshaw, where I rested myself till Friday, and then put myself on board the 'Corsair' at half past twelve; and although we had the wind right ahead, we had a very calm sea, and one of the best passages, for the distance, I ever had, either in these or any other seas. In fifteen hours I was completely across the channel; and, having dined in the one kingdom, I was long before breakfast time in the other. It was indeed a mercy that the passage was so short, for a worse set of passengers I never met with. They passed for, and affected to be, Irish gentlemen; and by their conduct seemed to be in league with hell and death, and with the devil to hold agreement—drinking, vociferating, arguing politics, in the most ferocious manner; talking high treason; abusing the king, the queen, the duke of

Wellington, and many others, in the most unmeasured manner; swearing, cursing, vowing the death of all the tithe proctors; one stated that he had engaged a man at half a crown a head to cut the throats, and take off the heads, of all and every of the tithe proctors that might show themselves on his estate. And to all this was added the vilest brothel obscenity. My heart was often obliged to say, 'Gather not my soul with sinners, nor my life with the blood thirsty;' and could say with one of old, 'O Lord, thou knowest I have not loved the company of the unrighteous in this world, let me not be condemned to have it eternally in the world to come.' To avoid these infernals, I walked the deck to a late hour, and then came down among them to lie upon a sofa, for I had no other bed. O what a hell to be condemned to keep company with such workers of iniquity! After such a companionship, what a blessing, on the following Sabbath morning, I felt the communion of saints to be! We had a lovely congregation at the chapel in this place, (Donaghadee,) and all appeared cordially to hear, and deeply to feel."

The conference of 1832 was held in Liverpool, at the time that the cholera was raging to an alarming degree. Though the doctor was in a very poor state of health, and was affectionately expostulated with by Mrs. Clarke not to go, he answered: "I know you never grudged me in my duty and work; and I think with you that I am scarcely fit to go. But I have duties to perform in reference to Shetland and the Irish schools: and, besides, I earnestly wish to leave my testimony for God and Methodism once more in the midst of my brethren." He attended; but, while there, wrote to a friend thus: "I have been variously afflicted, and, indeed, have been brought down almost to the sides of the pit, and, though much better, my health is in a great measure prostrated; and though I am here at conference, I am far from being in a state either to do or to attend to much business. I went to Ireland to work much, but I was called to suffer, not to labour. Indeed, I was overworked before I crossed the channel, and had little strength to lose when I got to the scene of my labours. Striving to do what I was not able to perform, I had four relapses. Well, in all these I was preserved from every murmuring thought. I knew I was in the hand of the Lord, and therefore was safe, and my expectation has not been disappointed; I feel that God alone is my portion. I write in conference, and have such a troublesome cough that I can scarcely write intelligibly, and must give it up." He, however, at the earnest request of his brethren, preached twice. His sermons will not soon be forgotten by those who heard them. After the conference he went to Frome, where his son Joseph was curate, to assist in the formation of a "Society for the Melioration of the Condition of the Poor" in that extensive parish. On the 19th of August he preached his last sermon at Westbury, near Bristol, from 1 Tim. i, 15: "This is a faithful saying, and worthy of all acceptation, that Christ Jesus came into the world to save sinners." On the 23d he safely arrived at home. At family worship he offered up his supplications in reference to the cholera, that "each and all might be saved from its influence, or prepared for sudden death." On Saturday, the 25th, it was observed by the family that he commenced his prayer with these words: "We thank thee, O heavenly Father! that we have a blessed hope through Christ of entering into thy glory." On rising from his knees, he remarked to Mrs. Clarke that he thought he must not kneel down much longer, as it was with pain and difficulty he could rise up again. In the evening he rode into Bayswater, at which place he was engaged to preach the following day. He appeared fatigued with the journey; and when application was made to him to fix the time for preaching a charity sermon, he replied, "I am not well; I cannot fix a time; I must first see what God is about to do with me." The next morning he was seized with cholera morbus, had just time and strength to declare that his trust was in Christ, and, about eleven o'clock the same evening, August 26th, 1832, he fell asleep in Jesus. On Wednesday, the 29th, his remains were interred in the burying ground adjoining the Methodist chapel City-Road. His grave is the next to that of Mr. Wesley. "Them which sleep in Jesus will God bring with him."

From the leading incidents in Dr. Clarke's life, as narrated in the preceding pages, the reader may obtain a tolerably correct view of his character, and cannot fail to perceive that the doctor was no ordinary man. We shall now briefly notice his peculiar characteristics. In his personal appearance there was nothing very remarkable. He was about five feet ten inches in height, and had rather a tendency, as he advanced in age, to a free habit of body. His frame was well compacted together, his limbs symmetrical, and his whole person remarkably erect. His eyes were small and brilliant, and of a light gray. His countenance was exceedingly rubicund; and his hair, when young, was of a reddish kind of yellow, but very soon assumed a silvery hue. His very walk was expressive of the buoyancy of his mind, and the whole of his features characteristic of the benevolence of his heart.

His understanding was clear, active, searching, and vigorous; formed for investigation, capable of grappling with any difficulty, remarkable for its patient application, and possessed a singular ability for arranging and generalizing subjects; perhaps more adapted for analysis than for synthesis. His powers of invention were fruitful, and his imagination vivid; but this faculty he neglected, rather than cultivated. His memory was surprisingly retentive, he states, indeed, that of the thousands of sermons which he delivered he never knew beforehand one single sentence that he should utter, and that this was owing to the verbal imperfection of his memory. But those who have been much in his company have been frequently struck with his powerful recollection, not only of a subject in the mass, but also in its minutest details. The multitude of books which he read, the manuscripts which he examined, the sermons that he preached, the sick whom he visited, the journeys that he performed, the committees which he attended, the public business in which he assisted, the private interviews that he granted, the many volumes which he composed and published, the thousands of letters which he wrote,—in addition to all his other duties as a Methodist preacher,—are proofs that his industry must have been unintermitted, and pursued with unexampled energy. At the commencement of his public life he wrote: "I am determined, by the grace of God, to conquer and die; and I have taken the subsequent motto, and have placed it before me on the mantelpiece: 'Stand thou as a beaten anvil to the stroke; for it is the property of a good warrior to be flayed alive, and yet to conquer.'" But, like Mr. Wesley, though he "was always in haste, he was never in a hurry." His dress, library, garden, farm, all showed him to be a man of order. What his hand found to do he did it with all his might, and he did it at once. To nearly every letter he replied by return of post. To idleness he seems to have had no propensity: in whatever company or situation he was found, even in his relaxations, his mind was occupied. While others slept or banqueted, or idled out their despicable days in gossiping and folly, he kept the glorious harvest of this issue full in view, and ploughed with all his heifers, reckless of the sun and rain. To a young man he says, "As a travelling preacher I learned more in one year than I learned before in many at school. The grand secret is to save time. Spend none needlessly; keep from all unnecessary company; never be without a praying heart; and have, as often as possible, a book in your hand. Make yourself master of Mr. Wesley's Works, and those of Mr. Fletcher and Mr. Sellon. Read over the Lives of the first Methodist preachers,—they are in the former Magazines;—and read the Journal of David Brainerd, Missionary to the North

American Indians; and 'the Saints' Everlasting Rest,' as abridged by Mr. Wesley. Do not lie long in bed, nor sit up late at night."

Doctor Clarke cultivated the useful rather than the ornamental arts. Of all the liberal arts he ever considered music as the least useful. The few first-rate poets he read with high relish. On those of a second or third order he seldom cast his eye. He possessed, in a high degree, the rare ability to use knowledge. He himself observed that the learning that is got from books, or the study of languages, is of little use to any man, and is of no estimation, unless practically applied to the purposes of life; and it is said by one who knew him well, that "there never was an individual who could use to such purpose all the stores which he accumulated. He possessed an astonishing power of gathering together rays of light from the whole circuit of his knowledge, and pouring them, in one bright beam, upon any point which he wished to illustrate or explain. And the treasures of knowledge which his unwearied industry had drawn together, were all made subservient to the more effective execution of his ministerial office."

His conversion, as we have seen, was clear, sound, and decided: of this, a life of uniform, practical, growing piety, covering over the space of more than half a century, is the delightful witness.

But the following testimony of the venerable Henry Moore, who knew the doctor longer than any man who survived him, must not be withheld: "Our connection, I believe, never knew a more blameless life than that of Dr. Clarke. He had his opponents; he had those that differed from him, sometimes in doctrine, sometimes in other things; but these opponents, whatever they imputed to him, never dared to fix a stain either upon his moral or religious character. He was, as Mr. Wesley used to say a preacher of the Gospel should be, 'without stain;' or, as a greater than he had said, Dr. Clarke could have said, 'Which of you convinceth me of sin?'" Like the patriarch, he said, "Till I die, I will not remove my integrity from me. My righteousness I hold fast, and will not let it go. My heart shall not reproach me as long as I live." Such was his unbending integrity that it may be said of him, as truly as it ever was affirmed of any statesman or patriot, "He would lay down his life for his country, and would not do a base thing to save it; one who would neither tread upon an insect, nor crouch to an emperor."

His attachment to Methodism continued to the last, and was then shown by a bequest for the relief of its chapels. He has been heard to say more than once, "I belong to the Methodists,—body and soul, blood and sinews. This coat" (seizing hold of his own sleeve) "is theirs." In a letter to me he remarks: "For nearly fifty years I have lived only for the support and credit of Methodism: myself and my interests, the Searcher of hearts knows, were never objects of my attention: I came into the connection with a single eye and an upright heart; and by the mercy of God I have been able to retain both." From censoriousness he was perfectly free. His judgment of his brethren was never harsh or severe. He was always ready to speak in their praise, and to put the best construction on their sayings and doings. His humility was deep and unaffected; with all his learning there was no parade. However familiar he might be among his friends, yet among the great and the learned he was modest to an excess. He shunned the gaze of the public, and preferred preaching in small chapels to large ones. He had a high sense of honour, but without pride and ambition. He would submit, with all cheerfulness, and without the least affectation, to perform the meanest offices for himself, his friends, or the poor. In a letter, dated Feb. 4, 1823, he writes: "Visit the people from house to house; and speak in the most affectionate manner to them. Take notice of the children; treat them lovingly: this will do the children good, and the parents will like it. Cheerfully partake of the meanest fare, when the people invite you. About two years ago, when travelling among the cottages in Ireland, I went into a most wretched hovel, and they had just poured out the potatoes into a basket, which, with a little salt, were to serve for their dinner. I said, 'Good people, will you let me take one of your potatoes?' 'O yes, sir! and a thousand welcomes, were they covered with gold!' The people were delighted to see me eat one, and another, and a third; and thought that I had laid them under endless obligation. But they thought me an angel when for every potato I had eaten I gave them a shilling. But they had no expectation of this kind when I first asked liberty to taste with them. Other clergy carry themselves *aloft* from their people, and thus assume and maintain a sort of anti-scriptural consequence. Methodist preachers have another kind of consequence—their humility, their heavenly unction, and the sound of their Master's feet behind them. Too much familiarity breeds contempt, but humility and condescension are other qualities."

His disinterestedness was beyond all praise. He never once used the influence which he possessed with some of high rank in behalf of himself or family. When he had the opportunity of reaping considerable emolument for his labours under government, and he was asked what they could do for him, he replied, "O, nothing; I dwell among my own people." He had also a kind heart: the various forms of human woe excited his softest sympathy. The distressed never left his door unrelieved. He has several times been known, when near his own gate, to give away his shoes in order to cover the feet of another. In the commencement of the year 1816, which was unusually severe, many hundreds of sailors were thrown upon the benevolence and compassion of the inhabitants of Liverpool: Dr. Clarke had some cottages untenanted, into which he put a quantity of straw and blankets, and then sent for twenty of the poor fellows. In the day time, they were employed in making the road to his house; and at set hours they assembled in his kitchen to their meals, one of the party having remained in-doors to cook for the rest. As a master he was, if possible, over indulgent. As a father, though he very seldom directly praised any of his children, he was notwithstanding passionately fond of them: and they, in return, were as fond of their father. When he heard his son Joseph preach the first time, he wrote to me in language which, perhaps, it would hardly be prudent to publish; but which fully exemplified the saying: "A wise son maketh a *glad* father." As a husband, he was just what a husband ought to be: he loved his wife, as Christ loved the church. As a friend, he was accessible, affable, communicative, obliging, faithful, and affectionate. It was, however, a maxim with him, that "proffered sympathy, in the time of deep sorrow and privation, whether it come personally or by letter, tends to exacerbate the evil which it wishes to remove." When I was deprived, by death, of a lovely son, he wrote to me thus: "I know well what it is to bury a child; for I have buried six: a *sympathizing* friend may say, 'Well! it is the Lord's will, and they are better provided for!' Thus I have learned that it is a mighty easy thing to bury *other folks'* children!" In every private relation of life he was an example worthy the imitation of all; nor was he less so in his *public character* as a minister of Christ.

Before I make any remarks on the doctor's preaching or writing, I will gratify my readers with a valuable letter of his to a young preacher, who had written to him for advice on the subjects of which it speaks:—

"MY DEAR BROTHER,

"I have given many general and particular advices to my younger brethren in 'A Letter to a Preacher on his first Entrance into the Work of the Ministry.' If you have not read this little tract, you should get it without delay. I would lay down two maxims for your conduct: 1. Never *forget* any thing you have learned, especially in language, science, history, chronology, antiquities, and theology.

2. *Improve* in every thing you have learned, and *acquire* what you never had, especially whatever may be useful to you in the work of the ministry. As to your *making* or *composing* sermons, I have no good opinion of it. Get a thorough knowledge of your subject: understand your text in all its connection and bearings, and then go into the pulpit depending on the Spirit of God to give you power to explain and illustrate to the people those general and particular views which you have already taken of your subject, and which you conscientiously believe to be correct and according to the word of God. But get nothing by heart to speak there, else even your *memory* will contribute to keep you in perpetual bondage. No man was ever a successful preacher who did not discuss his subject from his own *judgment* and *experience.* The *reciters* of sermons may be *popular;* but God scarcely ever employs them to convert sinners, or build up saints in their most holy faith. I do not recommend in this case a blind reliance upon God; taking a text which you do not know how to handle, and depending upon God to give you *something to say.* He will not be thus employed. Go into the pulpit with your understanding full of light, and your heart full of God; and his Spirit will help you, and then you will find a wonderful *assemblage of ideas* coming in to your assistance; and you will feel

the benefit of the doctrine of *association,* of which the *reciters* and *memory men* can make no use. The finest, the best, and the most impressive thoughts are obtained in the pulpit when the preacher enters it with the preparation mentioned above.

"As to Hebrew, I advise you to learn it with the points. Dr. C. Bayley's Hebrew Grammar is one of the best; as it has several analyzed portions of the Hebrew text in it, which are a great help to learners. And Parkhurst's Hebrew Lexicon exceeds all that ever went before it. It gives the *ideal* meaning of the roots without which who can understand the Hebrew language? Get your verbs and nouns so well fixed in your memory that you shall be able to tell the conjugation, mood, tense, person, and number of every word; and thus you will feel that you tread on sure ground as you proceed. Genesis is the simplest book to begin with; and although the Psalms are highly poetic, and it is not well for a man to begin to acquire a knowledge of any language by beginning with the highest poetic production in it; yet the short hemistich form of the verses, and the powerful experimental religion which the Psalms inculcate, render them comparatively easy to him who has the life of God in his soul. Bythner's *Lyra-Prophetica,* in which all the Psalms are analyzed, is a great help; but the roots should be sought for in Parkhurst. Mr. Bell has published a good Greek grammar in English; so have several others. The Greek, like the Hebrew, depends so much on its verbs, their formation and power, that, to make any thing successfully out, you must thoroughly acquaint yourself with them in all their conjugations, &c. It is no mean labour to acquire these; for, in the above, even one regular verb will occur up ward of eight hundred different times! Mr. Dawson has published a lexicon for the Greek Testament, in which you may find any word that occurs, with the mood, tense, &c. Any of the later editions of Schrevelius will answer your end. Read carefully Prideaux's History. The editions prior to 1725 are good for little; none since that period has been much improved, if any thing. Acquaint yourself with British history. Read few sermons, they will do you little good; those of Mr. Wesley excepted. The Lives of holy men will be profitable to you. Live in the divine life; walk in the divine life, Live for the salvation of men."

In this letter the doctor has given his own method of preparing for the pulpit, and of announcing the words of eternal life. In the year 1825 I had the pleasure to travel, in company with my venerable friend, from London to Liverpool, for the purpose of preaching in behalf of the Wesleyan Methodist Sunday schools. We lodged under the hospitable roof of W. Comer, Esq. On Sunday morning the doctor called me into his room, and, with his wonted affection, said, "Sammy, tell me what subject I shall take this forenoon." "Why, doctor, what sermons or skeletons have you brought with you?" "Skeletons!" said he, "I never write skeletons, nor have I one line of any kind with me." At this I expressed my surprise, knowing that he had to preach in Liverpool on the Sunday and Monday; at the opening of Brunswick chapel, Leeds, and another new chapel in Bradford, in the following week; and a missionary sermon in Lincoln, in his way homeward. He then said, "Read me a chapter." I took the Bible and read.—When I had got partly through the chapter, he interrupted me by saying, "Read that verse again; I think it will do." This was done, and in a short time we went down to breakfast. At half past ten I proceeded to Mount Pleasant chapel, and he to Leeds-street, where he delivered, from the text I had read to him, a sermon, as no mean judge informed me, of the highest order. Now this will help to put the matter on its proper basis; and unless the doctor's preaching be judged by the circumstances under which he appeared in the pulpit, justice is not done to him. The question is not, whether some preachers, by bending the whole of their strength for weeks or months to get up a sermon, and then preaching it again and again for many years, have not produced as finished a discourse as what the doctor in general gave; but it is, whether we have known any preachers, who, without having written a word, could go into the pulpit on the shortest notice, and pour forth such a torrent of important matter, and all flowing out of the text, as Dr. Clarke frequently did? I trow not. He might not in every instance please the admirers of "elaborate, artificial eloquence, of studied grace and euphony, of methodical exactness and imaginative brilliancy;" yet he possessed, beyond all doubt,—even if the unbounded popularity and success of fifty years, from the Norman Isles in the south, to the Shetlands in the north, were the only proof—the essentials of a great preacher. His matter was rich and various; his heart was fervid; and he excelled in the power of selecting from his stores, almost at once, the suitable materials for the instant occasion, which he poured forth with energy and freedom. His plan was to prepare his *mind,* rather than his *paper* of particular arrangements; to keep the fountain full, and he knew that at his bidding it would flow; and by his commanding genius he gave the proper measure and direction of the streams; while God accompanied his word with an extraordinary unction of the Holy Spirit. Dr. Clarke's preaching was chiefly expository. He endeavoured to explain the terms in his text; to ascertain the precise meaning of the Holy Ghost; and then to apply to the understandings and consciences of his hearers the hallowing truths thus discovered. His preaching, though argumentative, was decidedly evangelical. No minister ever lived, who gave a greater prominence in his discourses to the vital truths of Christianity, or who contended for them with more consistency and zeal. In all his ministrations, there was a constant reference to the divinity and atonement of Christ, to the doctrines of justification through faith in his blood, and sanctification through the all-pervading and all-purifying energy of the Spirit. The "illimitable mercy of Heaven," the universal redemption of mankind, and especially the witness of the Spirit to the fact of the believer's adoption into the family of God, and Christian perfection, were his favourite topics, those on which he laid the greatest stress; and he frequently said, that, if the Methodists gave up these doctrines, they would soon lose their glory. He had also a peculiarly happy method of describing the simple, adapted, expeditions terms of salvation; and was the honoured instrument of leading many a penitent sinner immediately to the Saviour. The religion which he recommended to his hearers was eminently of an experimental, practical, and happy kind; such as is felt in the heart, exemplified in the life, and causes its possessor to "rejoice in the Lord alway, and again to rejoice." And all his subjects he applied with peculiar faithfulness, point, and expressiveness. He was once preaching on the love of God to man, and toward the conclusion of his discourse he gave a sweep to his arm, drawing it toward himself, and grasping his hand, as though he had collected in it several objects of value, and then, throwing them, like alms, in the full bounty of his soul, among the people. "Here," he said, "take the arguments among you—make the best of them for your salvation—I will vouch for their solidity—I will stake my credit for intellect upon them. Yes, if it were possible to collect them into one, and suspend them, as you would suspend a weight, on a single hair of this gray head, that very hair would be found to be so firmly fastened to the throne of the all-merciful and ever loving God, that all the devils in hell might be defied to cut it in two." Nor was he ever "hard to be understood." A poor woman in Shetland unintentionally paid the following compliment to him. She had heard of his celebrity, and went to hear him at Lerwick. On her return home, she remarked, with great simplicity: "They say that Dr. Clarke is a learned man, and I expected to find him such; but he is only like another man; for I could understand every word he said."

In prayer Dr. Clarke was simple, spiritual, and

sometimes singularly ardent. He approached the throne of grace with a holy and reverential boldness, as if he were speaking to One with whom he was familiar, to One of whom he had an inexpressible estimation. His prayers "were literally collects, in which the whole collected meaning and ardour of his soul, for the time being, were darted forth at once."

Nor did the fervour of his love to Christ, and to the souls of perishing sinners, cool in the least, "as days and months increased." When he had passed his threescore years, he wrote: "O Sammy! how highly has God favoured you, to employ you in this work! How glad I should be to be your companion! *When I could,* I was a missionary; and many hardships have I suffered: and I feel the same spirit still. Chasms, and bogs, and woes, and men, and devils would be nothing to me: I have met *all such* in the name of Jesus, and have suffered, and have conquered."

And in another letter:—"Were God to restore me to youth again, I would glory to be your companion,—to go through your thick and thin,—to lie on the ground, herd with the oxen, or lie down on a bottle of straw, as I have been obliged to do in former times. I do envy you. Where duty is concerned, winds, waves, and hyperborean regions are nothing to me. I can eat even the meanest things—I can dine heartily on a few potatoes, and some salt, or half a pint of milk. I can wear a sack, if necessary; for fine clothing I never affected. The S. P. are all gentlemen. I thank God I bore the yoke in my youth. You do not take too much upon you. Somebody must work; the burthen is laid on you. If God spare life, I will stand by you: and he will, should he be pleased to take me."

The writings of Dr. Clarke are very voluminous; and for simplicity, perspicuity, and energy of style,—for various, extensive, and important information,—are, perhaps, not surpassed in this or in any other language. Few writers have more successfully conveyed "thoughts that breathe in words that burn." The measure of syllables, and the dance of periods, were beneath his notice. He never sacrificed sense to sound; but communicated, and that without laborious effort, the treasures of his mind to others, in words best adapted to convey his meaning and most likely to be understood. The same great truths on which he laid such stress in his preaching, are equally prominent in his writings. On the "five points," all his readers know that his views were similar to those of the celebrated Arminius, of whom he entertained a high opinion, and once said to me that "the British public was greatly indebted to Mr. Nichols for his excellent translation of the Works of that eminent divine," which he warmly recommended to his friends, at every convenient opportunity. On the leading subjects of revelation, the doctor spoke and wrote as one having authority. "For comprehension of thought, clear and forcible argumentation, and profound views of divine truth, some of his sermons," says an able reviewer, "are equal to the best of Farindon, Barrow, or South; but, on the subject of personal godliness, incomparably superior.

We know of no sermons in which so much learning is brought to bear upon the all- important subject of experimental religion." His "Bibliographical Dictionary," and "The Succession of Sacred Literature," display most extraordinary research and application, and form a cyclopaedia on bibliographical subjects, worthy the attention of every student in divinity. An uninteresting or unimportant volume, or even pamphlet, Dr. Clarke never wrote. But his chief work, that on which he spent a laborious life, and on which his name will descend to posterity with greatest lustre, is his "COMMENTARY ON THE HOLY SCRIPTURES." It is undoubtedly the most critical and literary, and at the same time the most spiritual and practical, of any work of the kind, that was ever published in any living language. The author had an indescribable method of simplifying his learning;

and hence it is difficult to say whether the Commentary is most read and valued by the learned or by the unlearned, by the prince or by the peasant. It is a river in which an elephant may swim and a lamb may wade. He has not, like too many commentators, "each dark passage shunned;" but has routed the enemies of revelation from every text in which they had endeavoured to trench themselves, and fairly met and satisfactorily answered their strongest objections. The late Rev. John Newton, calling one day upon the Rev. Eli Bates, and seeing the first part of Dr. Clarke's Commentary lying upon the table, happened to open it in the place where the doctor makes several calculations in reference to the size of Noah's ark. When Mr. N. had finished reading the criticism, he closed the book, exclaiming, "Thank God! I never found these difficulties in the sacred record:" to which Mr. Bates replied, "Yes, sir, you have found them as well as Dr. Clarke; but the difference is, you always *leap over them,* while he *goes through them."*

Dr. Clarke ever gave his opinion on what he conscientiously believed to be the mind of the Spirit, with "unflinching, uncompromising, unprevaricating honesty and faithfulness;" and when he has differed from commonly received notions, he has done it in the most modest, candid, and Christian manner. The following are the terms in which he speaks of himself: "Though perfectly satisfied of the purity of my motives and the simplicity of my intention, I am far from being pleased with the work itself. Whatever errors may be observed, must be attributed to my scantiness of knowledge. I do not pretend to write for the learned; I look up to them myself for instruction. All the pretensions of my work are included in the sentence that stands in the title: it is *designed as a help to a better understanding of the sacred Writings.*"'To the numerous pamphleteering and magazine writers that took up pen against him while his Commentary was in course of publication, his constant reply was: "I am doing a great work, so that I cannot come down: why should the work cease, while I leave it, and come down to you?" In a letter to the late Rev. Joseph Hughes he says, "I never wrote a controversial tract in my life; I have seen with great grief the provokings of many, and a thousand times has my heart said,

Semper ego auditor TANTUM, *nunauamque reponam, Vexatus toties?*

But my love of peace, and detestation of religious disputes, induced me to keep within my shell, and never to cross the waters of strife. I had hoped, as I was living at least an inoffensive life, not without the most cordial and strenuous endeavours, in my little way, to do all the public and private good in my power, I might be permitted to drop quietly into the grave. But this is denied me"

To some remarks of mine in 1825, he replied: "You say my notes on Isaiah are too short—I do not think so: on my plan they are as long as they should be. It would have been easy to have made them much longer. Jeremiah and Lamentations are just finishing at press. Ezekiel and Daniel are ready to go in, as soon as the others come out. And, if God spare life and health, the twelve minor prophets will be finished before next Christmas: so I see land at last in this long and dangerous voyage."

At the conclusion of the Commentary in 1820, he says, "In this arduous labour I have had no assistants; not even a single week's help from an *amanuensis;* no person to look for common places, or refer to an ancient author; to find out the place and transcribe a passage of Greek, Latin, or any other language, which my memory had generally recalled, or to verify a quotation;—the help excepted which I received, in the chronological department, from my own nephew. I have laboured alone for nearly twenty-five years previously to the work being sent to the press; and fifteen years have been employed in bringing it through the press to the public: and thus about forty years of my life have been consumed." The following observations which he made in a letter to a young friend, should be more publicly known: "Mr. Wesley's Notes on the New Testament are excellent and useful; and, were I not fully convinced in the fear of God of what I am about to say, I would not say it. I then say, Carefully read over my comment on the Scriptures. I wrote every page of it in reference to the ministers of the word of God, and especially those among the Methodists; and I know of no work, be it what it may, in which the doctrines of the Methodists are so clearly stated, illustrated, and proved." In this I heartily concur.

At an early age Dr. Clarke took for his motto: "Through desire a man having separated himself, seeketh and intermeddleth with all wisdom;" and I remember asking him, some years ago, if he would advise me to apply myself to the study of geology and mineralogy, when he promptly replied, "Yes; a Methodist preacher should know every thing." He not only possessed one of the most select and valuable libraries in the kingdom, but he made such use of his opportunities as but few persons have done. The stores of useful knowledge which he amassed were prodigious. The late Rev. Robert Hall pronounced him to be "an ocean of learning;" while another eminent Baptist minister says he was "unquestionably the most universal scholar of his age." He never sought, but rather shunned, literary honours; thinking himself to be undeserving of them: but learned and literary societies thought otherwise. He received, as we have seen, his diplomas of A.M. and LL. D. from the University and King's College, Aberdeen; and was successively elected president of the Liverpool and Manchester Philological Society,—member of the Oriental Sub-Committee of the British and Foreign Bible Society,—sub- commissioner of Public Records,—librarian of the Surrey Institution,—fellow of the Antiquarian Society,—member of the Royal Irish Academy,—member of the American Antiquarian Society,—member of the Geological Society of London,—member of the Royal Asiatic Society, and member of the Eclectic Society of London. But, in a letter to his friend Mr. Drew, he piously observes: "Learning I love,—learned men I prize,—with the company of the great and the good I am often delighted: but, infinitely above all these and all other possible enjoyments, I glory in Christ,—in me living and reigning, and fitting me for his heaven."

To slavery Dr. Clarke was a most determined foe, considering "it and all its appendages the first brood of hell." In politics he was a whig; but he very seldom looked over the pages of a newspaper. I was with him when be read the "Voice from St. Helena;" and shall not soon forget the terms in which he spoke of the treatment of the exiled emperor, and of the manner in which the last war was conducted. On several subjects both civil and ecclesiastical, which of late years have created no small stir, he wrote to me with the utmost freedom. These letters, for reasons which need not be mentioned, are not published in this memoir of my dear and venerable friend, whose face I shall see no more. To say that I esteemed, admired, and loved him, is saying but little: for my esteem, and admiration, and affection were such as I never felt for any other man; and I am constrained to add, "Take him for all in all, I ne'er shall look upon his like again."

He was a burning and a shining light; and thousands for a season rejoiced in his light. He suffered, from the shadow of death, a momentary obscuration, and now appears in that region where "they that be wise shall shine as the brightness of the firmament; and they that turn many to righteousness as the stars for ever and ever."

END

Look for other Heritage of Truth titles from Apprehending Truth Publishers.

Defining Biblical Holiness
The Works of John Fletcher
New Testament Holiness
The Way to Pentecost
The Path of Prayer
The Call to Christian Perfection
Christian Theology

Available at your favorite online bookseller or visit ATPublishers.com for more Christian titles for your edification.

www.ingramcontent.com/pod-product-compliance
Lightning Source LLC
Chambersburg PA
CBHW071410040426
42444CB00009B/2177